PARTIES

*T*HIS new magazine is published four times a year and covers every season and every party feature, whether it is a meeting of the bridge club, a birthday party for the children, a Fourth of July celebration, a shower for the bride-to-be, an engagement announcement, a Hallowe'en dance or a church supper—whatever the affair may be, "PARTIES" will help you make it a success in every way.

It will show you how to create the real party spirit; how to fill the evening with gay, happy surprises; how to make the occasion merry and colorful through novel invitations, decorations, costumes, games, interesting table arrangements, appropriate refreshments, favors and prizes. In fact, each issue will be a veritable storehouse of valuable ideas.

SPRING   ～   SUMMER

HALLOWE'EN AND HARVEST

CHRISTMAS AND NEW YEAR'S

Yearly subscription 75c.   Single copies 25c.

In sending your subscription please be sure to indicate the issue with which it is to start. Single copies and yearly subscriptions may be purchased from stationers, department stores and many drug stores or direct by mail.

～

Dennison Manufacturing Co.

FRAMINGHAM, MASS.

Stores and Service Bureaus

BOSTON, 26 Franklin Street   NEW YORK, 220 Fifth Avenue at 26th Street
PHILADELPHIA, 1007 Chestnut Street   CHICAGO, 62 East Randolph Street
LONDON, W. C. 2, 52 Kingsway

How to Decorate
HALLS · BOOTHS · AND
AUTOMOBILES

SECOND EDITION

Contents

CHAPTER ONE

Hall Decorations . . . . pages 2–14

CHAPTER TWO

Decorations for Bazaars . . . . pages 15–23

CHAPTER THREE

Decorated Automobiles . . . . . . pages 24–28

CHAPTER FOUR

Baby and Doll Carriages Decorated . . . pages 29, 30

CHAPTER FIVE

General Instructions for Handling Crepe
Paper . . . . pages 31–36

The illustrations and instructions in this book are planned to meet as wide a range of requirements as possible, but if you have a hall to decorate, the booths at a bazaar to plan or an automobile to make ready for a parade, and none of the many suggestions given here is adapted to your particular need, further information may be obtained by writing the Service Bureau at the nearest Dennison Store.

WILDSIDE PRESS

Chapter One

HALL DECORATIONS *for* MANY OCCASIONS

BRIGHT, colorful decorations create an atmosphere of gaiety and put people in a mood to be amused and entertained whether the occasion is a banquet, dance, bazaar or other gala event.

It is surprisingly easy to arrange effective decorations when crepe paper is the material chosen, because it can be utilized in so many different ways for friezes and for wall, stage, chandelier or overhead decorations.

When preparing to decorate be sure to have sufficient materials at hand. Estimate the required quantity as carefully as possible, for there is nothing more discouraging than to start a decoration and not be able to complete it as originally planned because of insufficient material.

For tools you will need a pair of large, sharp scissors, a hammer, plenty of pins, 2-oz. tacks, paste, wire and gummed cloth tape. If several people are working, be sure that each one is equipped with all the necessary tools in order to avoid the constant running back and forth with some article that two or three people need at the same time. Remember that all decorations are viewed at a distance and strive for effect rather than fine detail. Use large splashes of color whenever possible. If flowers are to be used, make them of exaggerated size with no detail except general shape and color and use an abundance of foliage.

The Color Scheme Is Important

THE main thing to consider when a hall is to be decorated is the color scheme and the principal units of decoration. The first impression as people enter the hall is the one to be considered. Therefore, the center chandelier, stage or balconies are naturally effective places on which to arrange the most elaborate decorations. The colors themselves are important. Is the decoration to be used in daylight or under artificial light? Try out the colors in the light before using.

Avoid the use of dark colors whenever possible, and if one must be used, combine it with a predominance of a lighter color.

Very much stronger colors can be used under artificial lights.

You cannot go wrong in choosing pink, yellow or lavender for your decorative scheme but blue, particularly the lighter tones, does not "light up" well and should be avoided for whole decorations. Blue may, however, if necessary to carry out class or college colors, be combined effectively with white and gold.

Bizarre effects that are so often required for Mardi Gras, Oriental and carnival decorations may well combine red, orange, yellow, jade green, purple, bright blue and violet with touches of black and gold.

The very nature of the occasion will almost always suggest the color combination to be used for the decorations. A Valentine party, for instance, demands red and white, while a child's party suggests pink or pink and white.

HAVE A CENTER OF INTEREST AND ALL THE REST A BACKGROUND

THE nature of your entertainment will determine the "center of interest." Whatever it may be, spend most of your efforts in making it effective and have all the rest of the decorations a background from which the main decoration shall stand out.

Decorations will be very much more effective if they are comparatively low rather than very high. This effect may be gained by the use of wires fastened across the hall or along wall spaces. To these wires, decorations such as streamers, festoons, pennants and banners may be fastened and effects achieved that could be gained in no other way.

Wooden or wire hoops suspended well below the chandeliers and decorated just as if they were around them will often solve a most perplexing problem when the light fixtures are in a very high ceiling. The decorations may be fastened to the hoops and the whole decorative unit put together in some convenient place, thus facilitating the work.

When the Stage Is the Center of Attraction

WHEN the stage itself is not to be used or if the orchestra is to be seated there, the principal decoration may often be arranged on it. It is very easy to transform the stage into a garden with flowers growing over a wall and gay butterflies and birds fluttering overhead.

The picture is easy to copy. If possible use real potted plants. When they are not obtainable, an admirable substitute will be found in crepe paper moss. It is really finely shredded crepe paper and is hung very loosely and irregularly over natural branches. By using different colors, the effect of leafy trees, brightly blossoming shrubs or snow covered branches may easily be obtained.

In the picture the picket fence is made of white cardboard cut in proper shape at the top. Below it, two strips of Decorated Crepe Paper No. 364, cut out along the top following the printed outlines of the flowers, are arranged one below the other. If the stage is to be entirely unoccupied this same wall effect may be repeated across the back.

Large banners or pennants may be hung at the front of the stage with streamers draped between them. The arrangement of banners and streamers shown on page 7 can be well adapted to a stage decoration.

THE LIGHTING FIXTURES ARE ALMOST ALWAYS DECORATED

THE separate light fixtures can be decorated so that they form the center of interest, and if several are trimmed alike with groups of streamers or festoons connecting them, wonderfully attractive results may be obtained.

Chandelier decorations can be fastened on wooden or wire hoops much more easily than they can be attached to the glass shades. Often, too, the chandelier is made up of a cluster of separate bulbs, in which case a hoop foundation is absolutely necessary.

Fringe is used extensively for chandelier decorations because the light shines through it so prettily and it may be so easily accommodated to the required depth.

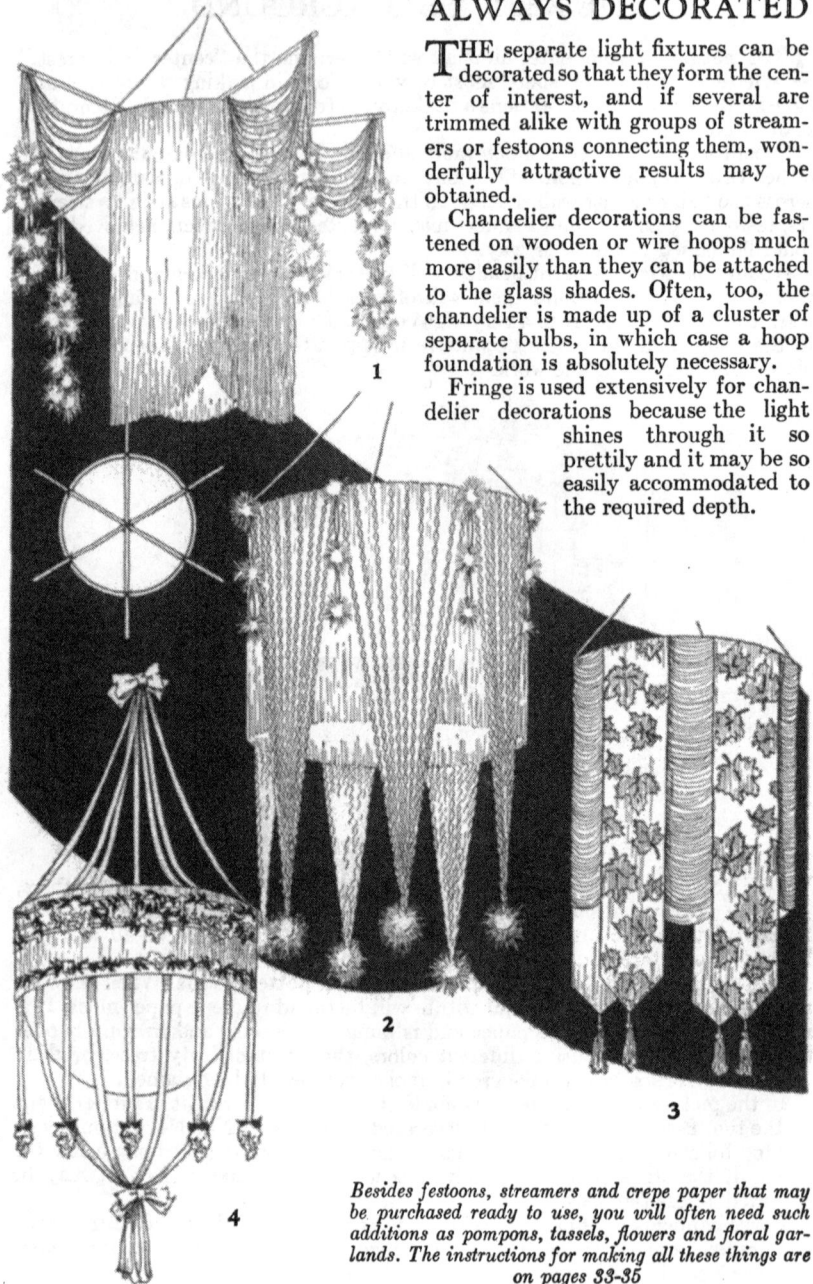

Besides festoons, streamers and crepe paper that may be purchased ready to use, you will often need such additions as pompons, tassels, flowers and floral garlands. The instructions for making all these things are on pages 33-35

The illustrations show how easy it is to obtain distinctly different effects.

Shades like these may be put together with surprising ease if the plain part of the fringe is pinned over the hoop.

No. 1. Make a soft fringe as described on page 32 and after it is in place, cross two or three flag sticks and fasten to the hoop. Attach pompons to the ends of the streamers that are looped and fastened in place as illustrated.

No. 2. After the fringe is arranged on the hoop, attach festoons all around at even distances. Twist them and gather together in groups, making four or six groups according to the size of the shade. Finish with pompons (see page 33).

No. 3. Fasten fringed drapery (see page 33) around the hoop and then add strips of Decorated Crepe Paper cut in pennant-like pieces. Tassels, made as described on page 33, may be added to the points.

No. 4. An easy way to make an effective decoration is to fasten a band of Decorated Crepe Paper around the light and then paste 2½ inch

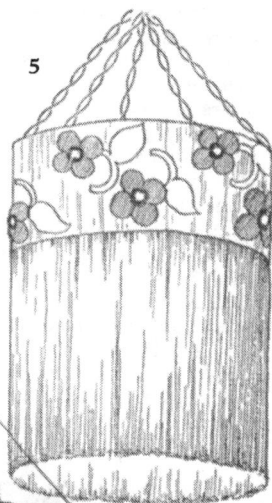

5

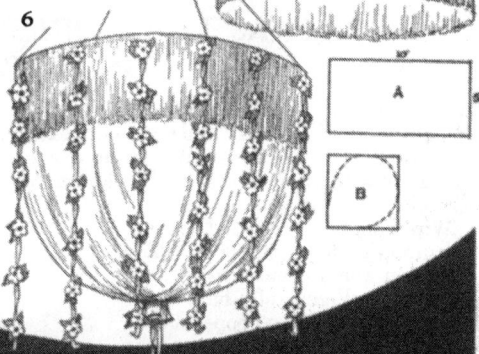

6

7

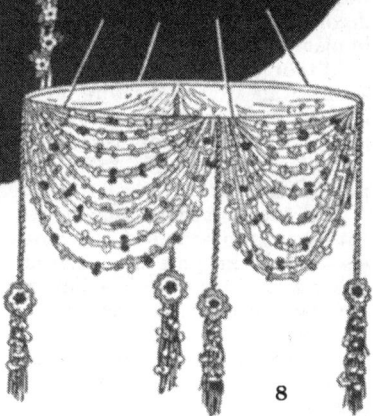

8

Almost all of these decorations can be adapted to any size from a shade for a single light that is not more than eight or ten inches across to a large center chandelier a yard or more in diameter

wide strips of crepe paper about four inches apart all around the lower edge. Alternately allow the ends to hang and be gathered together and fastened well below the light. The hanging ends may be finished with flowers, cut-outs or any preferred decoration.

No. 5.   For a very bizarre decoration, add a strip of plain crepe paper around the top of a fringed shade and paste large, brightly colored flowers to it. Make the flowers of 10-inch squares of crepe paper folded and cut as shown in diagrams A and B, page 5. Add a circle of a contrasting color for the centers and bright green stems and leaves.

No. 6.   When the light is to be softened, the crepe paper may be put straight around the hoop and gathered together at the bottom. The shade illustrated is brightened with dainty flowers cut from No. 952 Decorated Crepe pasted to narrow crepe paper ribbons.

No. 7.   Strips of crepe paper about 6 inches wide, cut across the grain and frilled on both edges, hang closely side by side around this shade. Large, flat flowers made of two sizes scalloped circles of crepe paper trim the bottom.

No. 8.   Strings of blossoms, made as described on page 35, that hang in several rows one below the other, can often be used to advantage around a large inverted glass globe. This arrangement is particularly desirable when it is not practical to lessen the light distribution.

PILLARS MUST OFTEN BE TAKEN INTO CONSIDERATION

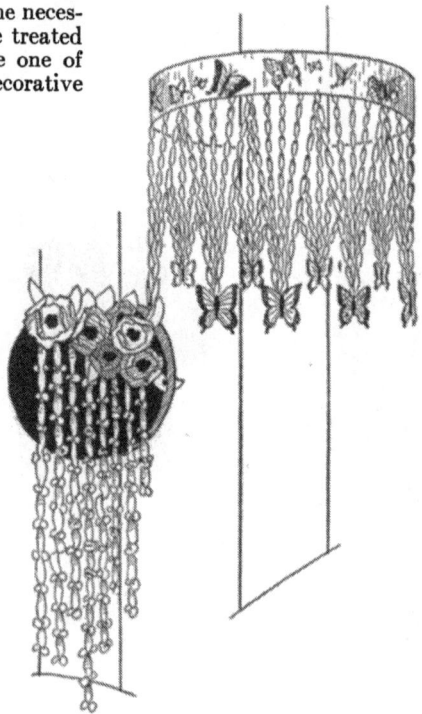

THE unsightly supports which are the necessary evils of so many halls can be treated in such a way that they will become one of the most attractive parts of the decorative scheme.

Wire hoops may be used to great advantage as foundations on which to fasten the various decorations. Fine wire will generally have to be used to hold both the hoops and the decorations in place because the pillars are almost without exception made of metal. Both of the decorations illustrated are fastened in place with wire.

At the right, festoons are attached at intervals around the wire hoop, twisted and fastened together in groups of three. A finish is made of butterflies cut from No. 313 Decorated Crepe Paper.

The other post shows a flat basket cut from cardboard filled with flowers. Two baskets are used, one on either side of the post. The flowers are made of circles of crepe paper scalloped on the edges. Hanging from underneath these flowers are floral vines made as described on page 35.

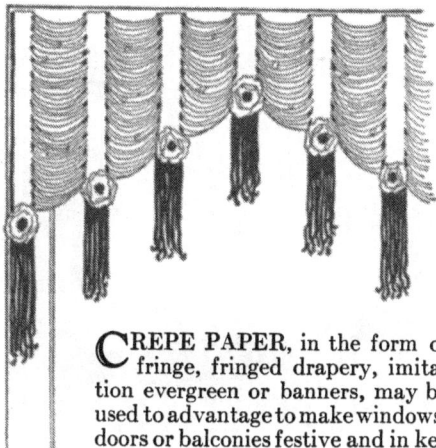

CREPE PAPER, in the form of fringe, fringed drapery, imitation evergreen or banners, may be used to advantage to make windows, doors or balconies festive and in keeping with the other decorations of a room.

Fringed drapery (see page 33), as shown above, may be used over a doorway or window. It is easy to arrange and it will accommodate itself to almost any required size. The picture shows an attractive finish of flowers and fringe.

Artificial evergreen (see page 35) is effective when used over doors and windows. Large flowers in vivid colors, as shown above, bring out the fresh, leafy green of the foliage.

A window drapery, when made of crepe paper fringe, will add a charming bit of color. The illustration at the right shows a few, large, flat flowers pasted to the fringe. For holiday decorations any suitable emblems such as hearts, shamrocks or pumpkins may replace the flowers.

Balconies may be easily brought into line with the other decorations. Banners with looped streamer drapery between them are always effective. The balcony itself may be covered with fringe or not as occasion demands.

For a more elaborate balcony decoration, the black and white

Continued on page 8

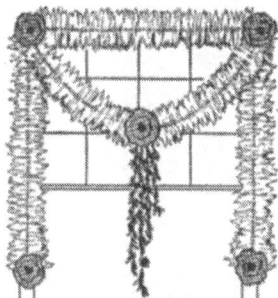

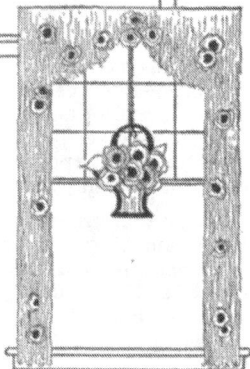

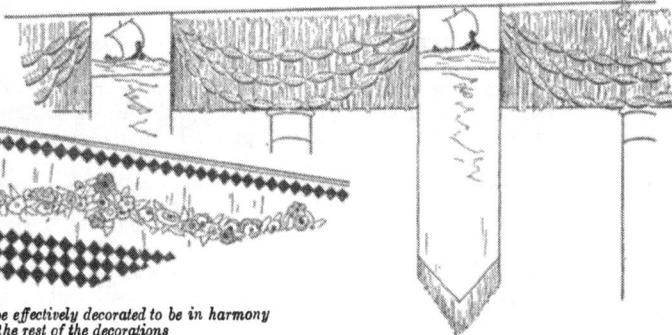

The balconies can be effectively decorated to be in harmony with the rest of the decorations

1

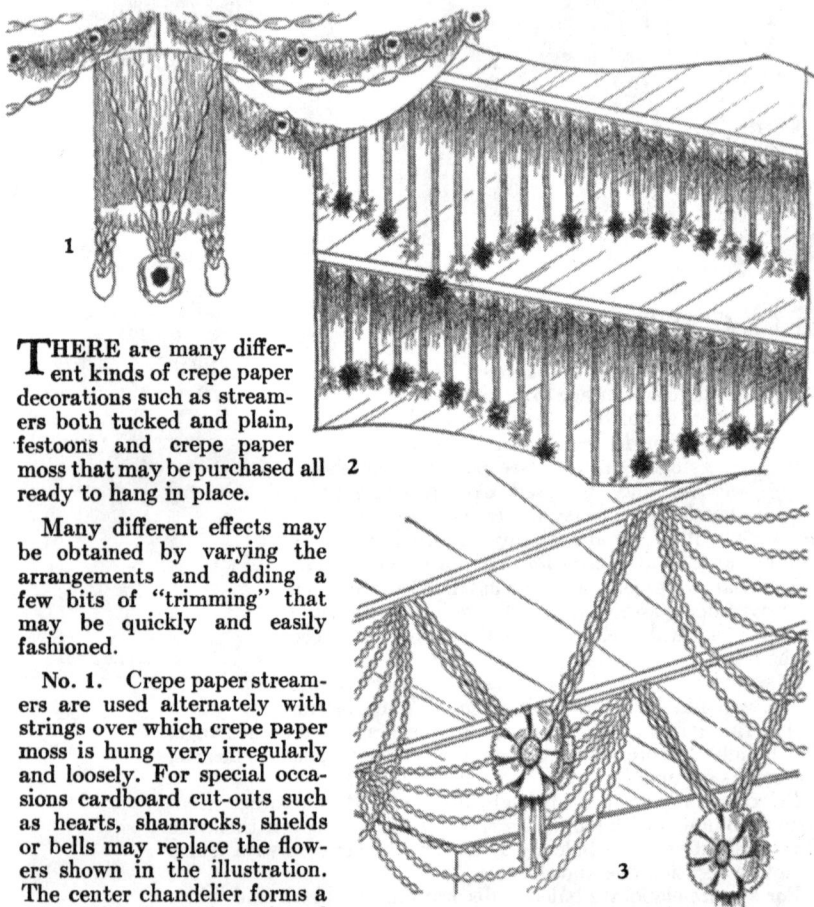

THERE are many different kinds of crepe paper decorations such as streamers both tucked and plain, festoons and crepe paper moss that may be purchased all **2** ready to hang in place.

Many different effects may be obtained by varying the arrangements and adding a few bits of "trimming" that may be quickly and easily fashioned.

No. 1. Crepe paper streamers are used alternately with strings over which crepe paper moss is hung very irregularly and loosely. For special occasions cardboard cut-outs such as hearts, shamrocks, shields or bells may replace the flowers shown in the illustration. The center chandelier forms a part of this decorative unit and **3** uses streamers and decorations to match those used among the moss.

No. 2. This arrangement of streamers is particularly desirable when there are cross beams in the ceiling. No. 2 Streamers are hung at intervals of about six inches. They may be perfectly even at the bottom or trimmed off so that they form a curved or pointed arch. Pompons or cardboard cut-outs may decorate the ends if desired or they may be left plain. In the illustration crepe paper

---

Continued from page 7

checked border and garlands of crepe paper flowers is extremely effective. The flowers are cut from variously colored crepe papers in scalloped circles and pasted to the plain crepe paper foundation.

OF BRIGHT COLOR OVERHEAD

moss draped over wire makes a soft finish at the top. This, of course, may be omitted.

No. 3. Tucked streamers, fastened at one end, twisted until they are round and fluffy, and fastened again as shown in the illustration, make an entirely different looking decoration. Groups of six hang one directly below the other in a long, graceful sweep, while between each group the low-hanging units make a center of interest. The large petaled flowers are made on cardboard foundations, the petals being pasted on both sides. Any appropriate emblems may replace the flowers.

No. 4. This effect is created by hanging a single thickness of finely slashed, fringed crepe paper (see page 32) over strings or wires. After the fringe is in place the lower edge is trimmed off to make it even and tapering to a narrower width over the chandelier. If the hall is large, festoons or streamers may fill in the spaces between the fringe.

No. 5. In this decoration the streamers go both ways at right angles to each other. Plain streamers are used parallel to the hearts and are twisted only slightly while those at right angles are Tucked Streamers which are well twisted. This gives an unusual and very attractive effect. Any suitable motif may be used in place of the pendent heart cut-outs that are used in the illustration.

No. 6. For a heavier decoration, green crepe paper may be made into imitation evergreen (see page 35) and used to drape the chandeliers and to hang in graceful festoons between them. To make this arrangement the most attractive, be sure to twist the garland well before the second end is fastened in place.

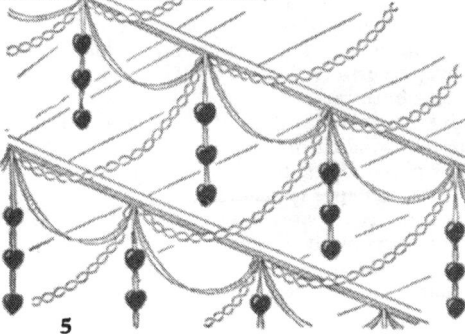

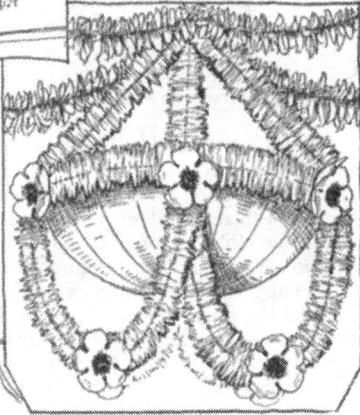

PERHAPS YOU MUST CREATE A
STAGE SETTING

WHEN school and other amateur plays are given, often there is no regular scenery for the stage. Indoor scenes can be easily accomplished, but out-of-door settings are not quite as simple. However, there is no reason why you cannot become a "scene painter." Crepe paper, cardboard, glue, paste, pins and unbleached cotton cloth are your "paints."

When you need a tree make one of a clothes tree, natural branches and crepe paper moss

Select simple scenes such as these and make no attempt to supply fine details

Do not try to make elaborate scenery. Remember that the audience is quite a distance away and strive for effect rather than fine detail.

Get the widest unbleached cotton and stretch it smoothly across the entire back of the stage. It may be necessary to make a light framework of wood to which the cloth may be tacked, or it may be arranged like a curtain with a strip of wood across the top and another at the bottom.

To copy the illustrations above, cover the cloth with light blue crepe paper, pinning the strips across the entire top, drawing them down like wall paper and fastening at the bottom. Use plenty of pins; they will not show at a distance.

Cut irregular shaped pieces of white crepe paper for clouds and pin in place. Make the trees, grass and other objects of crepe paper, crushing it before it is cut out (see page 33). Pin the different parts of the design in place first, then when you are sure that they are correctly spaced paste or glue if necessary.

It will often be helpful to sketch roughly the position of the trees, clouds and other objects with crayon.

BANNERS AND PENNANTS MAKE COLORFUL DECORATIONS

BANNERS and pennants are so simple to make and so extremely effective that you will wonder why you never thought of using them before. As a quick and "splashy" decoration nothing can surpass them. They may be hung in bare wall spaces, in windows, across the front of the stage and around balconies or hung at intervals through the center of the hall with groups of streamers connecting them.

To make a banner, use one or more straight 20-inch widths of crepe paper 5 to 10 feet long. Reinforce at one end by pasting the end over a small flag stick, narrow strip of cardboard or piece of wire. When two widths of crepe paper are required for large banners, the easiest method of joining the two pieces is to stitch them on the sewing machine with long stitches and loose tension.

Many times straight lengths of Decorated Crepe Paper may be used just as they are printed or a single motif may be cut out and pasted to plain colored crepe.

Plain or Decorated Crepe Paper or a combination of both may be used to make banners. Long, short, wide and narrow, they may be adapted to any size and shape

Page eleven

WHEN THE CEILING IS TOO HIGH TO DECORATE

SCHOOL gymnasiums, armories and similar buildings often present a problem from the decorator's standpoint because the ceilings are so high. An arrangement of streamers similar to the one illustrated here will often solve easily what seemed a hard problem.

The center of attraction is a large wire hoop from 36 to 48 inches in diameter, according to the size of the hall. It is suspended fairly low and decorated all around with strings of blossoms (see page 35, fig. 21). Make them about twice the size of the dimensions given in the instructions. Drape streamers from the top of the hoop to the chandeliers, balconies and sides of the hall. If the hall is large, two or even three of these hoops may be used.

The foundation of the chandelier decoration also consists of wire hoops. One should be about 12 inches less in diameter than the other. They are suspended by wires the required distance apart. The larger one is hung alternately with plain streamers and strings of blossoms. The plain streamers are looped and fastened to the lower hoop while the strings of flowers hang straight down. The streamers are caught together well below the second hoop and then fastened up so that a second looped effect will be obtained.

To arrange the streamers easily, select the number to be used in each group or section and gather the ends into a tight bunch. Fasten securely with wire by twisting wire around several times. Leave the ends long enough to fasten around the chandelier or other starting point.

A decoration similar to this is particularly effective when the streamers are any of the pale pastel tints, such as blue, pink, orchid or yellow and the flowers a variety of all these colors in deeper shades used hit or miss.

The cost of materials for decorating this hall is small indeed compared to the attractive results obtained. However, to create this charming setting you must be willing to spend quite a little time in making and arranging the decorations

BRINGING OUTDOORS INDOORS

FOR a more elaborate decoration, the hall may be transformed into an old-fashioned garden. Streamers, either sky blue or class colors, radiate in close canopy effect from a center point to all sides of the hall.

The walls are covered about five feet up with brick or stonewall design crepe paper, and below it, cut out following the outlines of the blossoms, is a row of old-fashioned flowers (Decorated Crepe No. 364).

Start working at the top of the wall and put the first strip in place. Cut off the plain narrow edge of the second strip. Paste or pin it in place below the first strip, matching the bricks as nearly as possible. Add another strip of the brick paper or the cut-out floral design as space requires. It will not be necessary to carry the brick all the way to the floor but only far enough so that it will be covered by the flowers. A "coping" is made of a strip of gray crepe paper.

A few stalks of pink crepe paper hollyhocks, used at the sides of doors and windows, will break any stiffness and also cover any ragged places.

Gateways may be made of cardboard or laths according to whether the entrance is a real one or just to make a break in the scenery. The instructions for arranging a stage background (see page 10) will be helpful if you wish to make a few trees in the background above the wall.

Instructions for making the stalks of hollyhocks are in the book,"How to Make Crepe Paper Flowers," referred to on the inside back cover

DECORATIONS FOR SCHOOL OR
CLASS DANCE

GYMNASIUMS and school halls must often be made festive for class or fraternity dances. Usually such festivities are dances, so that colorful overhead decorations are what will be most effective.

A canopy effect is extremely colorful and can be accomplished with comparatively little work. Wires are stretched across the hall, through the center and twice or more on either side. The center wire is the highest, the two on either side are about two feet lower and so on; the entire effect resembling a canopy. To these wires, crepe paper streamers are fastened in parallel rows. Pin the streamers over the center wire about four inches apart, twist and fasten over the succeeding parallel wires. This effect may be varied slightly by bringing groups of six or more together at the wall rather than continuing them in rows.

Large banners in class colors, made as described on page 11, will be very effective at intervals down the center of the hall, or if there are chandeliers at convenient heights they may be decorated as shown in illustrations 1 and 2 on page 4.

The stage may be entirely shut off with crepe paper fringe. Huge class letters and numerals are attached to the fringe. This fringe may be drawn aside during the evening if desired and an exhibition dance or some other special feature be staged.

It will take 8 dozen 2½ inch wide streamers to decorate a hall like this 25 feet by 50 feet.

Separate spaces are often arranged for the different fraternities. They should be decorated in the same style but if desired the society colors may be introduced in connection with the individual emblems

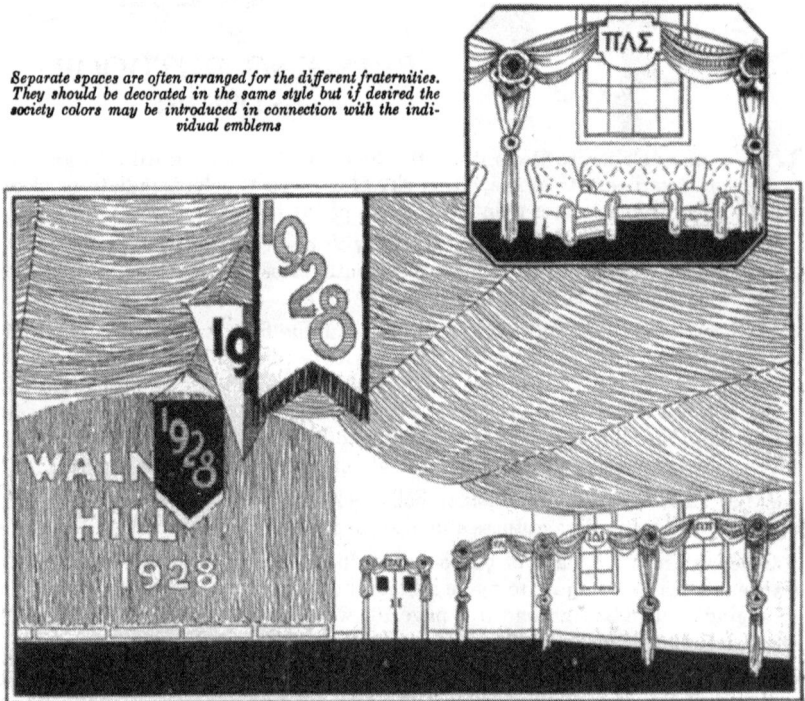

Chapter Two
PLANNING A BAZAAR

THE first thing to think about when a bazaar is being planned is the general decorative scheme. It must be appropriate for the hall in which the bazaar is to be held and the design and colors selected for each booth should, as far as possible, be in keeping with the wares that are for sale and harmonious with the booths on either side.

A "Flowerland Bazaar," each booth representing a different flower, can be carried out effectively, the flowers for each of the twelve months supplying the color scheme.

A "Snow Carnival" is appropriate for a winter-time bazaar. The colorings of the aurora borealis, snow and icicles supply the basic ideas.

The decorations of Japanese, Chinese and Oriental bazaars may be carried out in very charming ways.

A "Rainbow Bazaar" is very colorful. Each booth should have a "bow" over the top and the decorations around the lower part should vary in color with each booth, each being one of the different colors of the rainbow. The "pot of gold" and the gold coins with which it is supposed to be filled may be added (see page 17).

It is not necessary to spend extravagant sums for decorations in order to have them dainty and effective. By careful planning and co-operative buying the cost can be kept down to a very moderate sum. Estimate the quantity of materials required for each booth, then buy the materials for all of them at one time in order to get the benefit of any quantity prices. When only a part of a fold of crepe paper is needed for a booth divide it with another when possible.

When fringe, flowers and other decorations are to be made or the printed crepe paper designs are to be cut out, have them prepared in advance so that they may be assembled quickly when the framework of the booths is in place.

Have a decorating committee that shall be responsible for the actual putting up of all decorations. Rough sketches of all the booths will be helpful so that each worker may know exactly what the booths and other decorations are to look like.

Make the booths uniform either in size, color scheme or general arrangement and place them so that there will be plenty of space around them

HOW TO BUILD AND DECORATE A BOOTH

WHEN a bazaar is to be on an elaborate scale, the foundations of the booths are usually made for the occasion by a carpenter, but more often materials at hand must be utilized.

The Foundation

A BOOTH may be built on a regular table, "boards on horses" or even on an empty packing case. The most satisfactory size is six or eight feet long and 36 inches wide. Other sizes may be adapted to special designs (figs. 1 and 2).

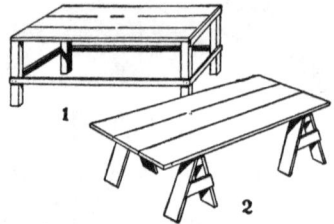

The Uprights

UPRIGHTS may be nailed to the four corners and cross pieces fastened between them (fig. 4). The addition of a roof effect (fig. 5) makes a more substantial foundation and will permit more elaborate decorations. There are many attractive ways to decorate a booth that has no uprights. Heavy wires, laths or bamboo strips may be fastened from the front corners to the opposite back corners and fastened together where they cross (fig. 3). Bamboo or wire arches can be used across the front or back. The Baby Booth, page 17, uses three such arches across the front of the booth.

Arranging the Decorations

FIRST cover the top of the table with white wrapping paper, allowing it to extend a little beyond the edges all around. Fasten under the edges with a few tiny tacks. Next arrange the decorations on the upper part of the booth and finally put the decorations around the lower part. Fringed crepe paper is very satisfactory to use; it does not tear easily and will stand a good deal of wear. Keep decorations around the lower part of the booth as *flat* as possible, because flowers, rosettes and pompons are easily knocked off in a crowded hall. As the paper is only 20 inches wide, it must often be pieced when it is used around the lower part of a booth. This may be done in two ways. A strip of wrapping paper about 18 inches wide may be fastened around the table and a frill of crepe paper wide enough to come down to the floor may be pinned to the lower edge. A wider ruffle can then be fastened around the edge of the table, as shown in the booth here. The second way is to sew two widths of crepe paper together on the sewing machine. Lay one piece on top of the other and stitch about one inch from the edge. Flute this double edge, then open out flat. Gather slightly along the top and fasten in place (see Toy Booth on page 19).

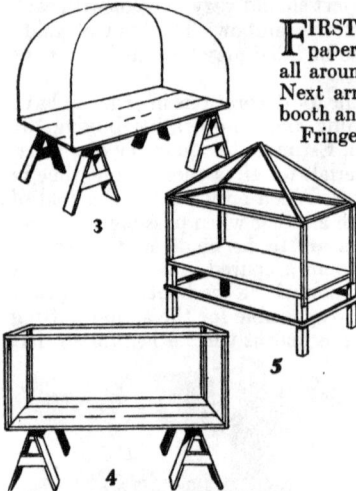

An easily arranged decoration that can be adapted to any special occasion by using appropriate colors and emblems

Cost of materials approximately $2.50 for booth 8 feet long

Fancy Work Booth

TO duplicate this design, cut a quantity of blossoms and leaves from No. 952 Decorated Crepe. Make "fringed drapery," preferably of No. 50 Baby Crepe, following the instructions on page 33, and also sufficient fringe to cover the lower part of the booth.

Tack the fringed drapery to the cross pieces at the top and to the sides. Gather the plain portions slightly to give the same effect as the illustration, then paste the flowers in rows to the plain part of the crepe.

Arrange the fringe around the lower part of the booth and finish with fringed drapery and flowers to match the top.

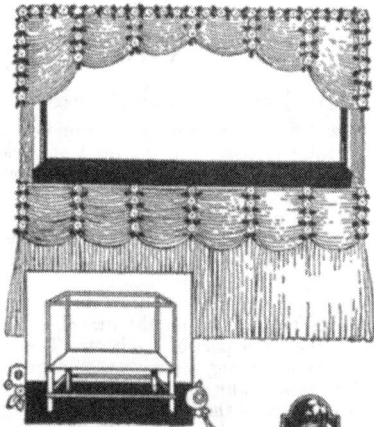

Approximate cost of materials $1.75 for booth 6 feet long

Baby Booth

THREE wire arches make this design possible. Fasten them to the table with double-headed tacks and tie together securely with fine wire where they separate. Wrap the wires with strips of crepe paper cut four inches wide and slashed on one edge into a fine fringe. After the paper is in place rough it up with the hands.

Cover circles of cardboard with various bright colors and suspend them as shown in the illustration, lettering them as required. The lower part of the booth is arranged as described on the preceding page.

Approximate cost of materials $2.50

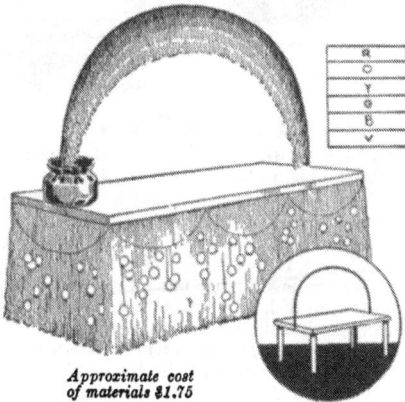

Rainbow Booth

TO make the "rainbow," cut pieces of Nos. 81, 65, 62, 43, 54, 23 three inches wide *with the grain* through the entire width. Paste them together, lapping one over the other about one-half inch in the order given above. (See diagram.) When dry fold *across the grain* and cut into a fine fringe (see page 32). Paste the uncut edge over the arch. Fasten a strip of cardboard around the wire to form the "pot" and cover it with gold paper.

Cover the lower part of the booth with fringed crepe in one of the colors of the spectrum. Disks of gold paper strung on gold cord may be added.

Approximate cost of materials $1.75

Bird and Flower Booth

IF the uprights are fastened to the middle of the table instead of at the front or back, the booth will look very different from an ordinary booth and with no extra trouble.

Branches in silhouette are made of black mat stock, and parrots, cut from Decorated Crepe No. 368, are mounted on cardboard and fastened to the branches.

A very quickly made flower, "mile-a-minute wisteria," is used on the branches and around the lower part of the booth. The instructions for making wisteria are on page 35.

Three thicknesses of fringe are used around the lower part of the booth. To make fringe see page 32. If it is made of No. 41 Green and the flowers are in shades of Violet Nos. 21, 22 and 23, you will have an unusual and very attractive color scheme.

Approximate cost of materials $2.50 for booth 6 feet long

Christmas Booth

A VERY simple but effective design that may be adapted to any special time or season by substituting appropriate emblems.

The wooden foundation must be made like the diagram and the festoons fastened to the top of the stick, twisted and fastened at even intervals across the front and sides.

A strip of Decorated Crepe is cut out and used as a finish at the top and around the table over a fringe of crepe paper (to make the fringe see page 32). The large bells and the star may be purchased ready-made.

Approximate cost of materials $2.50 for booth 48 inches in diameter

Approximate cost of materials $2.50 for booth 6 feet long

Hat Box Booth

THIS booth makes an attractive setting for hats, toilet goods or candy.

The foundation is a round table to which the uprights are fastened as shown in the diagram. The foundation of the "cover" is cardboard. If necessary reinforce it with wire.

For the lower part, paste the crepe paper to a strip of heavy wrapping paper the correct width and long enough to go around the table. Separate pieces of crepe paper are made to go from the bow at the top to the lower edge where they are fastened securely.

INTERESTING BY
UNUSUAL DESIGNS

Flower Basket Booth

TWO tables pushed close together with arches over all, as shown in the diagram, make a very satisfactory foundation for a large booth for fancy work or aprons.

Plain and Decorated Crepe Paper, joined together as described on page 16, is used around the lower part. A single layer of fringe cut in points relieves the plainness.

Flowers in dainty light colors, made as shown in fig. 21 page 35, are looped over the arches. The basket from the Decorated Crepe is mounted on cardboard and cut out. Strings of blossoms the same as used on the arches are added to the basket.

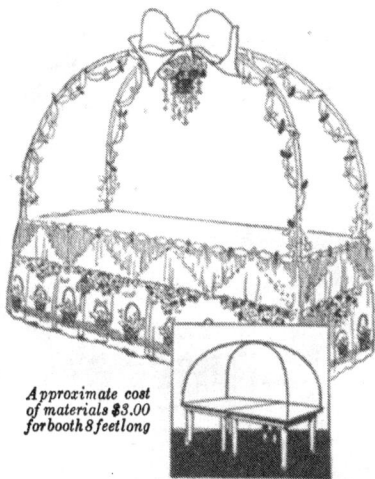

Approximate cost of materials $3.00 for booth 8 feet long

Approximate cost of materials $4.00 for booth 8 feet long

Toy Booth

MINIATURE Festoons in several bright colors make the clown possible. It is easy to see how they are fastened to the foundation. Put them in place first. Then add the face, hands and feet made of cardboard.

The ruffs are made of No. 380 Decorated Crepe Paper cut in points following the design.

Two widths of plain colored crepe paper are sewed together for the lower part. The stitching is done two inches from the edge, thus permitting a double frill to relieve the plainness of the lower flounce.

Garden Booth

THE awning may be made of Black and White Stripe No. BW 1, but if you must have another color combination you will have to add strips of color to a plain foundation after it is in place.

The lattice is made of strips of crepe paper cut three inches wide, stretched tightly and tacked in place.

The lower part requires Brick Design No. 916 and Old-fashioned Garden No. 368.

The instruction book, "How to Make Crepe Paper Flowers," gives patterns and instructions for making the stalks of hollyhocks.

Approximate cost of materials $3.50 for booth 8 feet long

Approximate cost of materials $2.00 for booth 8 feet long

Butterfly Booth

THE Butterfly Booth is made on a foundation that has uprights and heavy wire arch on the front.

For the butterflies, cut pieces of crepe paper about 20 inches long and 15 inches wide. Vary slightly to make different sizes. Cut the two opposite edges as shown in figure 1. Gather through the middle, fastening with wire, and pull the wings into shape as shown in fig. 2. Add a body made of black mat stock (figs. 3 and 4). The large butterfly is made in the same way, using two thicknesses of paper, one larger than the other.

The lower part of the booth is made as described on page 16, a piece of plain white being stitched to the top of the butterfly design.

Parrot Booth

THE coloring of this booth is very bizarre, black and white (Decorated Crepe No. BW 3) combined with vivid green, blue, purple, orange, yellow, and red streamers. You may use No. 3 Streamers or strips of plain crepe paper cut one-half inch wide.

The parrots, cut from Decorated Crepe No. 310, are mounted on cardboard and fastened to rings of black mat stock.

The gay streamers contrast sharply with the white fringed paper background.

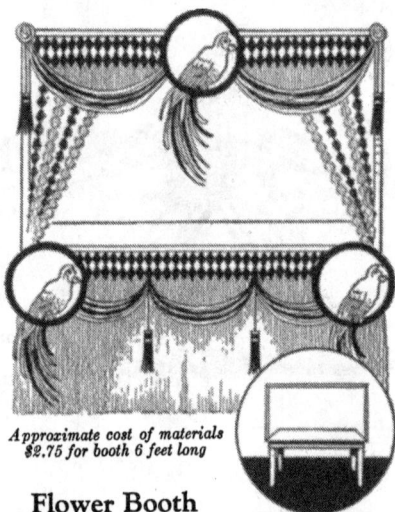

Approximate cost of materials $2.75 for booth 6 feet long

Flower Booth

TWO tables facing each other, with a flower-covered trellis at the back and on the sides, make an unusually attractive booth suitable for flowers, preserves or groceries.

The shelf may be made of boxes or boards fastened to brackets attached to the tables.

Autumn leaves on natural branches, rambler roses or morning glories are suitable decorations. (The instruction book, "How to Make Crepe Paper Flowers," gives instructions for making the flowers.)

The tables themselves and the shelves are edged with dark green fringed crepe paper behind which extra supplies may be hidden.

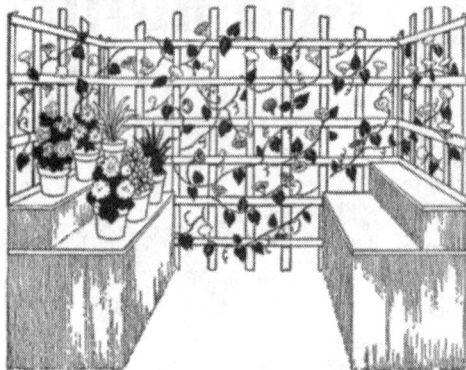

Approximate cost of materials $4.00 for space 6 yards square

Rose Trellis Booth

MAKE roses of several shades of pink, following the instructions on page 35. Make into a vine and twine it over the wire arches attached to the booth as shown in the diagram.

Cover the lower part of the booth with a flounce made of pink crepe paper and finish with a band of Decorated Crepe Paper in pink rose design, cut out irregularly along the lower edge of the design.

Other flowers, such as wisteria, morning glories, chrysanthemums or cosmos, may be used in place of the roses.

Approximate cost of materials $3.00 for booth 8 feet long

Candy Box Booth

TWO empty packing cases are ideal for the foundation of this booth, but if two tables are used heavy cardboard must be tacked around them to make a firm foundation. Smooth white or light colored paper is used to cover the foundation to represent the candy boxes. The "ribbon" may be any bright colored crepe paper.

Gather a strip of crepe paper about ten inches wide on the sewing machine for the frills at the top and paint the faces on circles of white cardboard. After they are completed cover with paraffine paper so that they will look like real lollypops.

Approximate cost of materials $4.00 for booth 8 feet long

Nosegay Booth

PINK, blue, violet, and yellow rosettes about 2½ inches in diameter, made as described on page 33, are fastened to pink crepe paper streamers and arranged as shown in the illustration. Pointed pieces of green are pasted here and there for leaves. More rosette flowers of the same colors are pasted to the centers of 12-inch lace paper doilies. The frill around the lower part of the booth may be either light green or white.

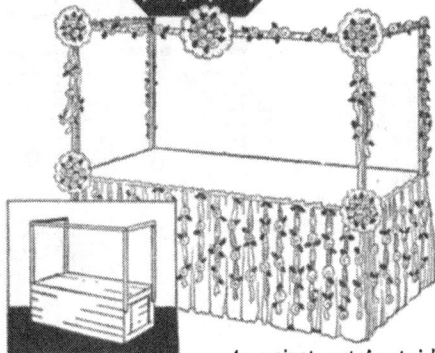

Approximate cost of materials $3.00 for booth 6 feet long

THE TEA ROOM ATTRACTS MANY PATRONS

THE space allotted to the luncheon or tea room is usually just a corner or space that is conveniently near the kitchen or serving room. If possible it is a good plan to have a temporary partition or railing erected. Both of the booths shown here are arranged in this way.

Booths at conventions and county fairs may be easily adapted from these two designs. For these only the fronts will have to be decorated.

Oriental Tea Room

DECORATED Crepe Paper No. 368 is arranged on a background of No. 70 Sand Crepe. Strips of orange and dark blue Streamers or Festoons extend at intervals to the top and to the floor. They are also used from the arch to the railing. The lantern is made of the Decorated Crepe pasted to a cardboard foundation.

By using Decorated Crepe Paper of appropriate pattern the same design may be very easily adapted to "The Parrot Tea Room," "At the Sign of the Bluebird," "The Black Cat" or "Grandmother's Garden."

The Japanese Tea Room

THE wisteria decorated pergola effect is created by making a "floral vine" such as described on page 35. using pieces of violet and purple twisted on strips of pale lavender. The uprights from which the vine and Japanese lanterns hang may be painted black or wrapped with strips of black crepe paper.

The lower part of the booth is made of "fringed drapery" (see page 33). Either lavender or pale yellow may be used. It will be necessary to use two widths, one pinned below the other.

NO BAZAAR IS COMPLETE WITHOUT "A GRAB"

Pierrot's Pockets. Sew two widths of No. 380 Decorated Crepe Paper together. Gather slightly on one edge and paste around the edge of a 20-inch cardboard circle. Add extra pieces, reinforced with wire around the top, for the pockets. Draw the whole thing up like a bag and stuff with crushed paper. Tie a head made of a clown mask to the top. A hat, pompons and a ruff of bright blue add the finishing touch. Articles of different prices may be in the opposite pockets.

Who'll Buy a Flower? The wearer of this fascinating costume goes about the hall, allowing anyone who will pay for the opportunity, a chance to unpin any flower he may select from the streamers of her dress. Numbered cards are attached to the flowers. Correspondingly numbered bundles should be spread out on a flower bedecked booth.

Over the Garden Wall. Cover a folding screen with No. 389 Stonewall Design Crepe Paper and arrange over it Decorated Crepe No. 364 cut out along the top edge. Add hats attached to sticks as shown in the illustration. The mystery packages are attached to the ends of numbered strings that hang over the top of the wall. Someone behind the wall may replace the strings as they are removed.

Robbing the Bird's Nest. Fasten a natural branch to the side of a wash tub or clothes basket. Pad the sides slightly with crepe paper and then wrap with brown crepe paper that has been stretched fully and crushed unevenly. Hang green crepe paper moss over the branches and fasten birds cut from No. 10 Decorated Crepe Paper among them. Fill the "nest" with packages wrapped to represent eggs.

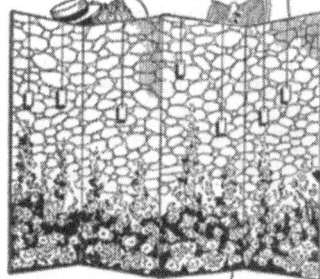

The Sugar-Plum Tree. Fasten natural branches to the pegs of a clothes tree. Wrap the tree with dark brown crepe paper to represent the tree trunk and drape green crepe paper moss thickly over the branches. Attach wires with hooked ends to the branches. The "sugar-plums" can be hooked on as needed. They should be wrapped in all sorts of bright colors.

Chapter Three

DECORATING THE CAR FOR PARADE OR FETE

ALMOST every community celebration includes among the gala events a parade, and its most attractive feature is the section of decorated automobiles.

There are usually prizes offered for the best decorated cars and there is almost no limit to the opportunities for creating original designs and color schemes.

An automobile is not an easy thing to decorate,

A good design for the car that is to lead a patriotic parade

principally because there are so few places that afford means of attaching the decorations. To overcome this difficulty and to keep the decorations from scratching the car, the body is usually covered with cambric or similar material. Put pieces over the hood and tie to the hood fastenings, then put pieces around the body of the car, tying, pinning or sewing in place as opportunity offers. Spool wire is easier to use than string when the cloth must be tied in place. It can be pushed through the cloth and fastened around posts or other projections and be held tightly in place with two or three twists.

Gummed cloth tape is also useful for holding the cloth in place when there seems to be no possible way to fasten it. The effect of the finished decoration depends largely on the tightness and smoothness of the cloth foundation, so be sure to arrange it carefully (fig. B, page 25). Sometimes decorations are arranged without a cloth foundation when a simple, quick decoration is needed. The decorations on the two cars illustrated here are put directly on the cars.

For a quick trim, paste yellow gummed circles back to back on white festoons, then twist them

When the body of the car is uncovered, natural green, flowers or tucked streamers may be used in just the same way as the "daisy chains"

THE TOURING CAR MAY BE DECORATED

Fig. A

Hold the petal between the thumbs and forefingers and twist toward you with one hand and away from you with the other

Twisted Petals, arranged tier upon tier, make a very attractive decoration. The strips of crepe paper should be cut about 10 inches wide and the petal divisions one inch wide and four inches deep. Twist each petal division as shown in the diagram. Pin or sew the strips of twisted petals to the cloth foundation, beginning at the bottom and working up.

The wheels are made on cardboard foundations (fig. A). When completed they are fastened to the wheels with wires thrust through the cardboard as shown in the illustration.

Rose Petals cut, curled and cupped as described on page 32 cover the entire car. The strips should be 10 inches wide and the petal divisions six inches wide. Separate roses are attached to the bamboo arches over the top. A solid color may be selected for the petals or a very pretty effect may be gained by shading them from dark at the bottom to very light at the top. The wheel decorations are made on cardboard foundations as described above.

Rose petals make a lovely decoration for an open car

Fig. B

Fringed Crepe works up quickly and is soft and fluffy. The crepe paper should be cut in strips about 10 inches wide through the entire fold and the slashes made about one-half inch apart *with the grain* of the paper. Flowers of any preferred variety may outline the top of the car and be used to make the required letters. The instructions for cutting fringe are on page 32.

DECORATIONS FOR THE CLOSED CAR

Rose Petals may also be used effectively on a closed car. Follow the instructions on page 25. The large roses are made on cardboard foundations similar to those used for the wheels. Although it takes double the quantity of material it will be very much more satisfactory if the rose petals are made of a double thickness of crepe. Two shades used together are very attractive. Decorations such as these often win the first prize.

Fringed Crepe for covering a car may be cut *across the grain* or *with it* but, whichever way is chosen, use several rows of short fringe rather than one deep one, because the wind will blow a deep fringe aside the moment the car is in motion and the whole effect will be spoiled.

The butterfly is crepe paper glued to a wire frame. This frame must be attached very firmly to the front of the car. Fine wires will have to be used from the tops of the wings to the front of the car as well as to and from several other points.

Crushed Crepe is excellent for covering the whole body of the car. The bluebirds shown in the illustration are cut from Decorated Crepe Paper and pasted in place. The large one is made on a cardboard foundation and covered with blue crepe paper. It is easy to use the small birds as models to copy.

Instructions for making rose petals, fringed crepe and crushed crepe are on pages 32 and 33

THE DELIVERY TRUCK IS OFTEN IN THE PARADE

TWO pieces of wall board cut in the required shape and two bamboo arches make it possible to make the truck look like this. Red, white and blue combined with other patriotic emblems are always to be desired but the same general arrangement may be used if the trade mark colors of some particular product are to be featured.

Be sure to take low hanging electric wires into consideration when you are planning a high decoration for a car or float

The design below requires a substantial framework of some kind. Several rows of short fringe, one below the other, are arranged around all four sides and artificial evergreen (fig. 22, page 35) is draped over it.

This is a splendid design to choose if you are going to feature some special machine or product. It may have the place of honor on the raised platform

WHEN A FIVE-TON TRUCK ENTERS THE PARADE

Pretty girls in fetching costumes help carry out the decorative scheme

A trellis work of laths arranged over a foundation of wall board, covered with crepe paper or painted, may be festooned with roses or wisteria. Bamboo arches, crepe paper fringe, Japanese lanterns and parasols complete the design.

Instructions for making either roses or wisteria are on page 35. It will take several hundred blossoms to cover a large truck. If possible use natural green as a foundation for the blossoms. Small branches of laurel or other evergreen may be wired to the trellis and the flowers in turn be wired to them.

A patriotic design is always easy to arrange on a truck that has removable sides. Use heavy wrapping paper as a foundation around the edge and glue or pin to it, one below the other, three ruffles of crepe paper gathered along one edge on the sewing machine. You will be well repaid if you reinforce each of the strips that extend from the stars to the body of the truck by stitching through the center on the sewing machine, using a long loose stitch.

A complete framework over all four sides will be necessary to carry out this design. It may be covered with fringed, crushed or crinkled crepe paper. If fringed crepe is used cut the paper in 10-inch strips and cut the fringe with the grain of the paper. Use at least two thicknesses of fringe; three or four will be better. The flowers are made as shown in fig. 18, page 35, except that they are much larger and not so pointed at the ends of the petals.

Chapter Four

DECORATED DOLL AND BABY CARRIAGES

WEE tots trudging along pushing gaily decorated doll carriages, or riding in their own daintily trimmed baby buggies, are always the center of attraction when a doll or baby carriage parade is a feature of a carnival or other gala event.

The carriages are treated just as if they were miniature automobiles, the body usually being covered with cloth as a foundation for the paper decorations. The wheels, too, are treated in the same way, the decoration being made on cardboard foundations that are fastened to the wheels with fine wire.

Practically all of the decorated automobiles illustrated may be simplified and adapted in miniature for doll or baby carriage decorations.

The Carriage May Be Decorated with the Top Up or Down

The two carriages illustrated show how the decorations may be adapted to use with the top either up or down. A patriotic design is always popular. To copy the picture, first cover the body of the carriage with cambric as described on page 24. Wrap two pieces of heavy wire with red crepe paper and attach to form two crossed arches. Cover the cloth foundation with white, crushed crepe paper (see page 33, fig. 10). Trim the arches with pendent stars, made by pasting two blue gummed stars together back to back with a piece of narrow blue ribbon between them, and flowers made of two scalloped circles of crepe paper pasted one on the other and pinched up a bit. Eagles, cut from Decorated Crepe Paper, tassels and more blue stars complete the decoration.

The "proud mother" is dressed in red, white and blue crepe paper to carry out the color scheme.

Roses, jonquils, daisies, sweet peas or poppies may be used to carry out the dainty design on the right. The foundation is crushed crepe paper over a cloth foundation. The color selected may vary with the flowers to be used but you will make no mistake in choosing a soft shade of green.

The instruction book, "How to Make Crepe Paper Flowers," gives complete instructions for making all of these flowers

A LL of these decorations may be adapted for either baby or doll carriages. Be sure to cover the body first very tightly and smoothly with cambric and attach all other decorations to this foundation.

No. 1. The May Basket is easy to copy. Attach straight laths to the front and back of the carriage and then fasten cross pieces to them. Wrap with narrow strips of crepe paper and add flowers and ribbon bows. Gather frills of crepe paper on the sewing machine and pin or sew to the cloth foundation.

No. 2. The Boat. Gaily fluttering pennants and flags are appropriate for the ship of which a tiny lad is the "captain." The lower part of the carriage is covered with rows of crepe paper fringe. Use strips of paper five inches wide and cut the fringe *with the grain*.

No. 3. "Dr. Stork" requires a wire foundation. This frame and the rest of the carriage are covered with white, crushed crepe paper. A similar effect may be obtained by using two silhouette birds like those shown on page 28.

No. 4. Fluffy Frills and dainty flowers in pink and white make a charming background for a sweet, wee, golden-haired baby. The picture is easy to copy.

No. 5. A Child's Cart is the foundation of this design. Pieces of cardboard are tacked to the sides. The rose petals and fringe can be easily glued to them. The wire arches are arranged and decorated as described for booth decorations on pages 16 and 19.

Chapter Five

GENERAL INSTRUCTIONS

BEFORE starting to decorate have all materials at hand as well as scissors, hammer, tacks, pins, paste and wire. If possible have such things as cut-out designs of Decorated Crepe Paper, fringe and pompons prepared in advance ready to assemble.

Work for effect, do not putter over details. Get the general decoration finished, then if time permits, add fine touches. Remember that the decorations must come down and use the smallest tacks that will hold (2 oz. or 3 oz. are the best) and drive them in only part way. Wire is better than string for attaching decorations. Two twists hold securely when string is apt to slip and be hard to tie. Gummed Cloth Tape may sometimes be used for holding decorations in place when nothing else seems to "work."

Plain crepe paper is almost always stretched a little before using. This should be done by two people. First double the ends over once or twice, or better still roll them around rulers or sticks so that they will not tear, then pull steadily until the paper is sufficiently stretched. When Crepe Paper, Festoons or Streamers are to be tacked up, fold one end over about one-half an inch two or three times *with the fold on the outside*, then tack in place.

To Cut a Strip of Plain Crepe Paper. Slip the paper partly from the packet. Measure the required width. Run two or three pins straight through the packet and the paper to keep it from slipping, and using the edge of the packet as a guide, cut through the entire thickness (fig. 1).

Fig. 1

To Join Two Widths of Crepe Paper. As the crepe paper is only 20 inches wide, and for a flounce it must be used with the grain running up and down, often two widths must be pieced together. Lap one piece flat over the other about one-half an inch and either stitch on the sewing machine or paste.

Crepe Paper May Be Sewn either by hand or on the sewing machine. The sewing machine can be used to good advantage for sewing two widths together, gathering ruffles, sewing up seams and sewing on bands. It is not always necessary to gather the paper with needle and thread; it can be gathered up with the fingers and a wire twisted tightly around to hold it.

Fig. 2

Fluted or Ruffled Crepe Paper. Hold the edge of the paper between the thumbs and forefingers of both hands as shown in the illustration. Push away from you with one hand and pull toward you with the other. Move the hands a little and repeat until the entire strip is fluted (fig. 2). The paper may be fluted before it is removed from the packet. Slip it partly from the packet and stretch all thicknesses at once.

To Cut Decorated Crepe Paper. Always remove the wrapper from Decorated Crepe Paper before cutting it. When cutting it in straight strips unfold and refold, then cut, marking if necessary. When the designs for borders are to be cut out better results can be obtained if the printed outline is not followed too closely, particularly if it is very irregular. Cut all outlines in curves rather than in sharp points. Remember that for all decorations the design is viewed from a little distance and fine detail of cutting out will not show. It is much quicker to cut the curved lines than the sharp points.

Pointed Petal Edge. Cut a strip of crepe paper the desired width. Place the fore and middle fingers of the left hand on the edge of the crepe paper, holding it securely. Hold a pencil with an eraser in the right hand and with the eraser end push the paper down between the fingers as shown in fig. 3. Move the fingers along a little and repeat until the whole strip is pointed. This petal edge is often used for decorative purposes instead of strips of rose petals. The effect at a little distance is very similar and it may be made more quickly than the curled rose petals.

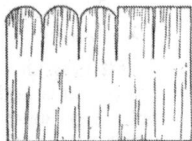

Fig. 3

Strips of Petals. Cut the paper the correct width through the entire fold (fig. 1, page 31). Unfold, stretch slightly and, starting with the two ends together, refold until there are eight thicknesses. Make straight slashes along one edge the desired depth and distance apart. Round off the corners as necessary. Be sure to leave a piece of paper at the bottom an inch or more wide uncut (fig. 4).

Fig. 4

Twisted Petal Edge. Cut strips of petals as described above, then holding a petal division between the thumbs and forefingers of both hands, twist toward you with one hand and away from you with the other. Repeat until the whole strip is twisted (fig. 5). Very attractive two-color effects may be gained by folding, cutting and twisting two contrasting colors together. Another variation is made by cutting oval pieces of crepe paper of contrasting colors about the shape and size as the tip of the petal

Fig. 5

division. Place one of these oval pieces on each petal division before it is twisted. It will not be necessary to paste; the twist will hold the two pieces of paper together securely.

Rose Petals. Either strips of petals or separate petals may be shaped in the same way. Roll the two top edges of each petal over a steel knitting needle of suitable size and if a crushed effect is wanted push the crepe close together as it is rolled around the needle. Several thicknesses of petals may be curled at the same time (fig. 6). When very large petals are being made, use a pencil instead of a knitting needle.

Fig. 6

Cupped Petals. Take several thicknesses of petals together, or single petals, and with the thumbs on one side around the petal and the forefingers on the opposite side near the edge, push the petal out into a cup shape (fig. 7).

Fringed Crepe Paper. For decorative purposes almost all fringe is cut *across the grain* of the crepe. Strips of fringe 20 inches long and any depth up to the whole 10 feet of the fold may be made. Unfold, stretch and cut off pieces the desired depth for the fringe. Fold up the lower edge to within an inch or two of the top. Redouble several times, then, beginning at the right hand end, cut the fringe as fine as desired, cutting through all the thicknesses, but leaving the one-inch heading at the top uncut (fig. 8). Shake out, then stretch. Crush the cut strips between the hands. Shake out again, fold over the uncut edge once or twice and with the fold on the outside tack the strip in place. If necessary use more than one

Fig. 7

Fig. 8

thickness. Even off the lower edge after the fringe is in place. When more than one thickness is used, fold the pieces together before tacking in place.

Fringe that is to be used for flower centers and for some other purposes is cut *with the grain* of the crepe.

Fig. 9

Fringed Drapery. Slip a fold of crepe from the packet and without unfolding it make slashes from one edge across the fold to within about two inches of the opposite edge. Make the slashes about one-half an inch apart. Unfold and use as required. Strips only 20 inches deep may be made, so that if it is necessary to have deeper for a curtain effect, two or more pieces should be pinned together, one below the other. Pin the plain portions together after the first piece is in position. Do not try to piece together before putting up (fig. 9).

Crushed Crepe. First stretch the crepe as much as

Fig. 10

possible, then lay it on a flat surface and take up a small portion in the tips of the fingers of both hands, crushing it tightly. Repeat until the whole piece is crushed (fig. 10).

Crinkled Crepe. Remove the paper from the packet. Roll round and round a

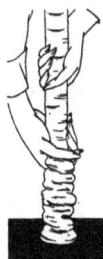

round stick of suitable size (a broomstick is just about the right size). Place the end of the stick against some firm object and push the crepe down very hard. Begin near the bottom and push down a small section at a time. Repeat until the entire width is crinkled. Slip the paper off the stick and unroll it (fig. 11).

Fig. 11

Pompons. Pompons may be made of Festoons, or crepe paper may be cut in strips of about the same width and slashed on both edges. Use a piece of Festoon about two yards long. Gather up into a tight bunch (do not roll it round and round) and twist a piece of fine wire tightly around the middle. Double together through the center, then with the tips of the fingers push the pompon into shape and if necessary clip off the ends to make the pompon round (fig. 12).

Rosettes. Cut a strip of crepe paper about the width required for the diameter of the finished rosette. Double through the cen-

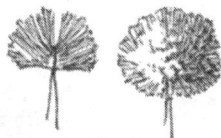

Fig. 12

ter lengthwise, being very careful not to make a crease on the doubled edge. Fold the left-hand end of the strip down diagonally. Gather the paper around this, holding it tightly at the bottom and wrapping it round and round and gathering slightly at the same time, until the correct size is obtained. Cut off and fasten tightly with spool wire (fig. 13). If

Fig. 13

necessary cut off any surplus paper below the fastening. Instead of fastening the rosette with wire it may often be held in the hand and then fastened in place with the same tack that holds it in the required position.

Tassels. Tassels may be cut either *with* or *across* the grain of the crepe. Stretch the paper well and cut pieces twice the length needed for the finished tassel. Double lengthwise through the center and cut as described for fringe on page 32, leaving the doubled edge uncut for an inch and a half or more. Use a strip of fringe 18 to 24 inches long, according to the size desired for the tassel. Slip a piece of fine wire or string into the folded edge and gather

Fig. 14

the paper up on it tightly and tie. If the tassel is to be used on the end of a cord, the end should be placed inside the tassel as it is being tied. Tie again below the first fastening, stuffing with a little soft paper if necessary to make the ball the correct size. Large tassels require more than one double thickness of paper. The strips should be folded one inside the other before they are folded and cut (fig. 14, p. 33).

To Wrap a Wire. The crepe paper for wrapping wires should be cut across the grain through the entire fold. The width will have to vary with the size and use of the wires, from one-half to two inches wide. When wires for flower stems and long heavy wires are to be wrapped the paper should be doubled lengthwise through the center before the wire is wrapped. Put a little paste on the end of

Fig. 15

the wire, then place the strip of crepe paper on it diagonally. Turn the end down over the wire and holding the wire in the right hand twirl it round and round. At the same time, guide the paper with the left hand, slanting it down and stretching it so that it will wrap the wire smoothly. As the winding proceeds, put the single leaves or groups of leaves in position on opposite sides of the stem, if they are to be used, the required distance apart. When the end of the wire is reached cut off the paper and paste the end in place. When it is necessary to add wire to lengthen stems, place the wire to be added beside the one being wrapped, allowing the wires to lap two or three inches and continue wrapping with the paper.

It will not be necessary to twist the two pieces of wire together. When flower stems are to be wrapped, put a little paste on the base of the flower or calyx and wrap the strip of paper around very tightly two or three times, then slant the paper down and proceed as described above (fig. 15).

To Wire Petals or Leaves. Use straight wires, not spool wire, unless the petals are

very small. Cut the wires a little longer than the petals which are to be used. Hold about six wires by one end, keeping them out in a flat row, not in a bunch. Rest on a piece of paper on the table, then cover the upper side of the wires with paste. Place the wires sticky side down, one at a time, in the center of a petal or leaf, allowing the extra length to project below the base. Press down firmly until dry.

Fig. 16

Electric Light Shades. The use of simple shades over electric bulbs will often so emphasize a color scheme as to make a decoration seem quite elaborate when really it is very simple.

The petal shade is adapted to many uses. Cut six petals about seven inches long and 4½ inches wide at the widest point, the shape of the diagram. Wire each through the center (see fig. 16). Glue six petals evenly spaced around an asbestos ring that can be purchased ready for use. Green crepe paper cut to resemble a calyx and wired or not as preferred may be added.

Glue a second asbestos ring on top of the petals and place under a weight to dry. When dry bend the petals in shape (fig. 16).

Sometimes it is not convenient to remove the glass shades from the lights. Wired petals made as described above may be glued to a narrow cardboard band and tied around the glass shade. Another quickly made shade that can be used on lights that hang down can be made of fringed crepe paper. Cut a circle

Fig. 17

or square of cardboard the required size and cut a hole in the center large enough for the bulb.

Glue an asbestos ring on both sides of this opening. Glue two or more thicknesses of fringe, cut as described on page 32, around the edge. Trim the lower edge off evenly (fig. 17).

EASILY MADE FLOWERS FOR DECORATING

Decorative Flowers. Cut strips of crepe paper the desired color six inches wide through the entire fold. Make into rows of petals (fig. 4, page 32), making each petal division 3 inches wide and shaped like the diagram. Make a center by cutting a No. 112 Festoon through the center lengthwise and gathering a piece 18 inches long into a tight bunch. Fasten tightly with spool wire. Gather a strip of five petals around the center and fasten in place with wire. Make the petals cup shaped as shown in the diagram. If necessary wrap the stem with green crepe paper (fig. 18).

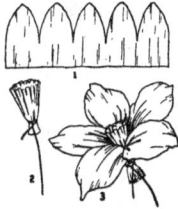

Fig. 18

Roses. Cut petals the shape of the diagram, making approximately the size indicated. While the petals are still in several thicknesses, curl the two top edges of the petals at both ends (fig. 6, page 32). Make both ends cup shaped (fig. 7, page 32). Separate the petals and double one petal through the middle, gathering together and wrapping one around the other just a little. Add another double petal, arranging so that the petals will come just between the first ones. Fasten with spool wire leaving sufficient length for the stem. If necessary add a calyx cut from green crepe paper and wrap the stem (fig. 19).

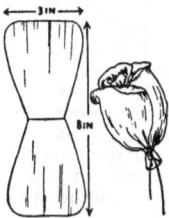

Fig. 19

Mile-a-Minute Wisteria. Cut strips of crepe paper through the entire thickness of the fold one-half inch wide. Before unfolding it, flute both edges (fig. 2, page 31). Unfold and make loops, having the longest about twelve inches long. Make the others of slightly irregular lengths and gradually shorter. If desired use two or three different shades in one flower, having the longest loops darker. Gather into a tight bunch and fasten tightly with spool wire. Add foliage as required. About two ten-foot strips will be required for each flower (fig. 20).

Fig. 20

Decorative Floral Vine. Cut and flute strips of crepe paper as directed. Cut oval shaped petals of crepe paper about two inches long and one inch wide, with the grain of the crepe going the long way of the petal. Hold one of these petals on top of the strip so that the grain of the paper is at right angles to the strip. Give the strip a complete turn, twisting it tightly. Add more petals, spacing them somewhat irregularly from one to two inches apart. The strips of crepe paper may be green and the petals assorted bright colors, or the strips may be a lighter tone of the color being used for the blossoms (fig. 21).

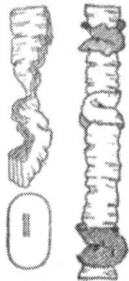

Fig. 21

Crepe Paper Evergreen. Cut strips of No. 46 Leaf Green Crepe Paper 8 to 10 inches wide through the entire fold. Cut each strip into points 3 inches wide and 2½ inches wide, making the points alternate rather than exactly opposite. Gather through the center on the sewing machine and then cup the petal divisions (see fig. 7, page 32).

Fasten one end in place, then holding the other end firmly, twirl until full and fluffy (fig. 22).

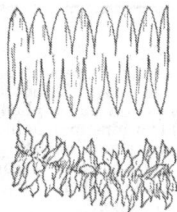

Fig. 22

Mounted Crepe Paper Figures.

Figures and other designs that are printed on Decorated Crepe Paper may be cut out and reinforced with either cardboard, wire or both. To mount on cardboard, cut the design out roughly (Fig. 24-A), then spread paste on the cardboard that is to be used and place the crepe paper on it, pressing it down carefully. Rub *with the grain* of the paper not *across* it. In order to prevent curling, another figure or a piece of crepe of harmonizing color should be pasted on the reverse side. Place under a weight to dry,

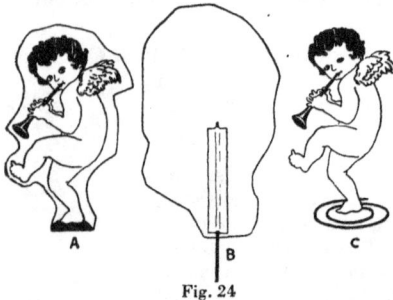

Fig. 24

then cut out, following outline of design.

If the figures are to be made to stand, before pasting the crepe on the back attach a piece of wire to the cardboard with gummed tape, allowing sufficient wire to extend below the base either to make a spiral standard (Fig. 24 B-C) or to be thrust through and fastened to another piece of cardboard that acts as a base. Use either No. 7 or No. 15 Flower Wire according to the size of the figure (Fig. 24 A-B).

Instead of mounting figures on cardboard, they may be reinforced with wire.

Sometimes two figures are used, a little cotton batting or crepe paper moss being

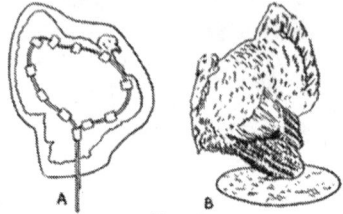

Fig. 25

used to stuff them slightly (Fig. 25-A). Often the designs required are printed on the crepe paper in such a way that one of them must be used wrong side out. If it is necessary to have both sides of the figure practically alike, the design that is wrong side out may be brightened with sealing wax or water color paint (Fig. 25 A-B).

Small flying birds and butterflies are often reinforced with wire. (No. 10 Flower Wire is the best size.) Cut out the figure following the printed outline. Measure the distance from the tip of the top wing on one side to the tip of the bottom wing on the other side. Cut off two pieces of wire this length. Lay one piece across the other at right angles in the middle and twist two or three times. Apply paste to one side of the wires and place on the figure, pressing firmly until dry. Bend the wings in correct position (Fig. 26 A-B-C).

Fig. 26

Many varieties of Dennison materials are required for the decorations illustrated in this book. The Crepe Paper is the most important item. The plain colors of Dennison Crepe are made in 47 different shades, while among the Decorated Crepe more than 88 different patterns can be supplied. Both the plain colors and decorated designs are packaged in folds 10 feet long and 20 inches wide. Dennison Crepe costs 15c. the fold in most shops, while the Decorated Crepe Paper will cost more, from 25 to 35c. the fold according to the design.

Festoons and Streamers of varying styles and lengths cost from 75c. to $3.00 the dozen.

Crepe Paper Moss, which is used for many decorative purposes, usually sells for 10c. a 2 oz. tube.

Wire is a very important accessory and may be purchased from 10c. for a 10-yard spool of fine wire to 35c. or 40c. for a dozen yard lengths of heavy weights.

Cardboard is needed for making many things. It may be had for about 15c. a sheet 22 x 28 inches.

The prices of all materials will vary in different localities and will be higher on the Pacific Coast and in Canada.

A detailed Price List of all Dennison decorative materials will be sent free on request. Stationers, department stores and many druggists carry Dennison goods.

BUY FROM YOUR LOCAL SHOPS

No. 526-25M-7-29   Printed in U. S. A.

INSTRUCTION BOOKS OF DENNISON CRAFT

*W*HEN you need decorations for a bazaar, dance, party, wedding festivity, automobile parade or celebration of any kind, when you need a fancy costume or when you desire to present a personally-made gift, you will find the Dennison Instruction Books of great help. The titles give only a hint of their helpful contents. They are:

How to Make Crepe Paper Costumes
How to Decorate Halls, Booths and Automobiles
How to Make Crepe Paper Flowers
Sealing Wax Craft
Weaving with Paper Rope
How to Make Table Decorations and Party Favors

Price, 10 cents each
Set of six books, 50 cents

❦

Dennison Service Bureaus

In order to give more explicit instructions and suggestions for the use of Dennison materials than is possible in our Instruction Books service Bureaus are maintained in the five Dennison Stores, where information will be given free of charge to all who call or write.

❦

Dennison Manufacturing Co.

FRAMINGHAM, MASS., U. S. A.

Stores and Service Bureaus

NEW YORK, 220 Fifth Ave. at 26th St.   PHILADELPHIA, 1007 Chestnut St.
BOSTON, 26 Franklin Street   CHICAGO, 62 East Randolph Street
LONDON, W. C. 2, 52 Kingsway

No. 526

www.ingramcontent.com/pod-product-compliance
Lightning Source LLC
Chambersburg PA
CBHW031617040426
42452CB00006B/574